PORTRAITS OF THE ENGLISH
VOLUME III

IN SICKNESS AND IN HEALTH

Selections from

HEADS OF THE PEOPLE
or
PORTRAITS OF THE ENGLISH

Drawn by Kenny Meadows
with Original Essays by Distinguished Writers

Edited by
Audrey Collins

HERITAGE BOOKS
2011

HERITAGE BOOKS

AN IMPRINT OF HERITAGE BOOKS, INC.

Books, CDs, and more—Worldwide

For our listing of thousands of titles see our website
at
www.HeritageBooks.com

Published 2011 by
HERITAGE BOOKS, INC.
Publishing Division
100 Railroad Ave. #104
Westminster, Maryland 21157

Other Heritage Books by the author:

Atlas and Guide to London, 1896, with Street Index
Portraits of the English, Volume I: Parish Characters
Portraits of the English, Volume II: Law and Order
Portraits of the English, Volume III: In Sickness and in Health
Portraits of the English, Volume IV: The Army and the Navy
Portraits of the English, Volume V: Working Lives
Portraits of the English, Volume VI: Country Lives

First published by Robert Tyas, 50 Cheapside, MDCCCXL

International Standard Book Numbers
Paperbound: 978-0-9536461-2-8
Clothbound: 978-0-7884-8781-1

CONTENTS

FROM THE PREFACE TO 'HEADS OF THE PEOPLE - PORTRAITS OF THE ENGLISH' 1840

'English faces, and records of English Character, make up the present volume. Leaving the artist and the writers to exhibit and indicate their own individual purpose, we would fain dwell awhile in the consideration of the general value and utility of a work, the aim of which is to preserve the impress of the present age; to record its virtues, its follies, its moral contradictions, and its crying wrongs. From such a work, it is obvious, that the student of human nature may derive the best of lore; the mere idling reader become at once amused and instructed; whilst even to the social antiquarian, who regards the feelings and habits of men more as a thing of time, a barren matter of *anno domini,* than as the throbbings of the human heart and the index of the national mind, the volume abounds with facts of the greatest and most enduring interest.'

INTRODUCTION

The chapters reproduced here have been copied in full from the original, with only minor alterations to layout and punctuation. The original spelling has been retained.

'HEADS OF THE PEOPLE' was published in 1840, as a two-volume set, edited by Douglas Jerrold, who also contributed several chapters. The aim was to entertain the reader, but the authors also claimed a 'moral seriousness of purpose' in portraying the many faces of the English, with their faults as well as their virtues.

THE APOTHECARY

He knew the cause of every malady
Were of of cold, or hot, or moist, or dry

CHAUCER

THE APOTHECARY

BY PAUL PRENDERGAST

STUDENT of character! behold our original! — the connecting link between the professor of physic, and the dealer and chapman — the ambiguous animal, the bat, the duck-billed platypus, the Siren Lacertina, the iethyosaurus — the Apothecary or medical man. Like the last-mentioned creature, he may become, in future times, one of an extinct species; but his resemblance will go down to posterity on the opposite page. Observe the results of a successful practice of pharmacy, and of the knowledge of human nature, in the exuberantly pendent cheeks, the amplitude of the abdominal curve, and the loose, easy suit of sober black, which, combining comfort with respectability, outvies the propriety of costume exhibited by the most affluent undertaker.

The Apothecary is a vendor of medicines, under the pretence of treating disease. Our countrymen are remarkable for an amiable weakness; a certain tenderness of pocket, which makes them endeavour to get everything at as low a rate as possible, not excepting medical attendance. For this reason, the majority of them intrust their health to the guardianship of the Apothecary, without entertaining the illiberal question whether, when he charges nothing for his advice, he does not rate it at its real value. Neither do they suspect that to pay a practitioner by taking his pills, draughts, and boluses, is no great temptation to him to abridge the complaints under which they labour; but with that common sense which, equally with generosity, so greatly marks their dispositions, they estimate the severity of a malady by its duration, and remunerate their attendant accordingly. They have also much faith in the virtues of drugs, and this usually in proportion to the nauseousness of their flavour, so that if the assistance which they derive from the Apothecary may with justice be called 'cheap and nasty,' the truth of the latter epithet enhances, rather than otherwise, the merit of the former. Such, too, is the discordance, both of opinion and practice, amongst the cultivators of the healing art, that it has probably been found by experience, that

7

remedies are just as efficacious: when administered from custom, or caprice, as when principle presides at their selection. The Apothecary is indebted, moreover, for his social existence, not only to the public, but also to the physician, whom he frequently 'calls in;' sometimes because it is unfashionable to die without the sanction of that functionary; sometimes at the patient's request; and sometimes because it is now and then expedient to shift the responsibility of a case.

Mr. Luke Label, whom we select for description, is a man of middle age, and of large business; a 'respectable practitioner,' as he is called whenever there is occasion to mention his name in the newspapers. His presence is portly and imposing, and is rendered so by the self-complacency engendered by success in life, the confidence acquired from long experience, and the sense of personal importance arising from the nature of his calling. Old and middle-aged ladies call him a 'fine man,' but whether by reason of his physical appearance or professional skill, or of prepossessions derived from the one in favour of the other, it is difficult to determine. His education, general and medical, was of an average kind; he was brought up at a third-rate school, where he learned 'little Latin and less Greek,' or rather, no Greek at all; and he studied medicine behind a counter. His therapeutical knowledge extends to the determination of the problem: 'Certain symptoms being given, what is the usual remedy?' All ulterior research he stigmatises as being 'speculative,' 'theoretical,' and 'visionary' — words which he has picked up in the course of his reading; he attaches the same meaning to all three of them, and applies them indiscriminately to any attempt to conduct a case upon philosophical principles. He aims at nothing but relieving a symptom; the cause of the disorder very possibly remaining untouched; — but what then? The sooner does the patient believe himself well, the more skilfully does he consider

8

himself treated; and the more speedily will his malady return; to the no small encouragement of pharmacy, and the infinite emolument of its professor. The strongest mental faculty of our pharmacopole is common sense, in the ordinary acceptation of the term; namely, a tendency to concentrate every thought and feeling upon one object — getting money. He has become, in virtue of this quality, a prosperous gentleman; past the necessity of announcing his occupation by an open shop, a gilt lettered board entitling it 'Medical Hall,' by a coloured lamp over the door; and the inscriptions, 'tooth-drawing,' 'bleeding,' 'cupping,' 'leeches,' and 'physicians' prescriptions accurately prepared,' displayed in the window. He is now installed in a house, which once belonged to a gentleman, in the neighbourhood of one of the squares; he has a brass plate, with his name upon it, on the door, and there is nothing else about his domicile to tell the world he is an Apothecary, but three large bottles, red, blue, and green, which peep, coyly and modestly, above the wire-gauze window-blind. His wide and lucrative field for exertion is situated in the genial regions of the west; where, in addition to the gluttony which produces nine-tenths of human ailments, a thousand injurious habits increase and diversify disease; where imaginary complaints are added to those which are real; and where scientific humbug is fostered by fashionable ignorance. He keeps his carriage, and a handsome one too — at least as handsome as a medical man's carriage can be; and he has attained to the highest honour of his craft, having lately been made one of that enlightened and scientific body — the Court of Examiners, at Apothecaries' Hall.

'Well!' said Mr. Label one day, as he stood in his shop with his back to the fire, 'a pretty good morning's work, certainly — yes, certainly. Twenty patients at three draughts a day — that's five shillings. Five times twenty, a hundred — very good. They'll take them for a week at least; seven times one, seven — thirty-five pounds — capital! Confound those people in St. James's Street; they *will* take pills; let me see — three at night and one in the morning, — four. Why, it will be a week before they take two boxes — we can't send more, — and that will be only two shillings. They might as well have washed them down with a little *haustus effervescens:* stop! — I know! — we'll leave out the *aromatic*, and then they'll get tired of them. Mr. Jackson.' The address to the apprentice was spoken aloud — the soliloquy was *sotto voce.*

'Yes, sir.'

'Leave out the *oleum cinnamomi* in Mrs. Tenderly's pills.'

'I did that the other day, sir, with Miss Diggram's, and she said they pained her.'

'You're a foolish fellow, sir! Do as I tell you. Is Miss Diggram Mrs. Tenderly?'

'No, sir.'

'No, sir? To be sure not. Don't constitutions differ, sir; and don't I know when they do and do not?'

'I should think so, sir — that is — of course. I suppose, though, they were pretty much the same in the twenty patients that you have ordered those draughts for.'

'Why, sir? what makes you say that?'

'Because they are all alike: *magnesiæ sulph,* two drachms; *compound tincture of lavender,* drachms three; and the rest water.'

'The rest *what,* sir?'

'Water, sir.'

'Mr. Jackson, I beg you'll mind what you're talking about. Water! Suppose any of the patients heard you; call it *aqua destillata* another time, sir. It's a very bad habit to get into an unprofessional way of talking. What do you think that Lady Mary Croakham would say if she knew that *pil: panis* meant bread pills?'

This was a question not meant to be answered; it obviously admitted but of one reply, which might have savoured somewhat of disrespect, if it had been uttered aloud. So Mr. Jackson, pausing before he spoke just long enough to shew that he had taken his master's hint, merely said, as he invested the last of the twenty draughts with the customary red paper head-gear and packthread cravat,

'We're out of corks, sir.'

'Are we? I'll send for some more, directly. What are you about, Mr. Jackson?'

'Capping, sir.'

'Capping! - do you call that capping? Look here, sir; this is the way — there — and don't go about complaining that I give you no professional instruction. Isn't this instruction? Unless you cap your draughts properly, who will ever take them but a pauper! Young men are getting above their business; they don't pay half enough attention to these kinds of things. Why, before I had been apprenticed two months, I had learned the whole art of dispensing in all its branches.'

This was quite true. Mr. Label had become, very early in his noviciate, a proficient in the art of pharmacy. His skill extended to every kind of manipulation, from the simplest pounding to the most elaborate pill-grinding; he could guess at all doses with exactness, from a grain to a pound, and in making up a pretty-looking draught for a fashionable invalid, would display more taste than the most imaginative confectioner.

'No, Mr. Jackson,' resumed the Apothecary, softened a little, as he reflected on his own capabilities; 'depend upon it, that to succeed in practice you must please the eye.'

'It's a rather difficult thing, though, sir, for a young man to get into practice in these times,' sighed Mr. Jackson.

'Eh! — why — not so very, if you go the right way to work. The first thing that you should do when you've passed, is to take a small business, with retail annexed.'

'Ah! I suppose so, sir. Draw it mild at first, and come it strong by-and-by.'

'Don't learn to talk in that kind of way, Mr. Jackson. I observe it's very much the rage with you young men just at present. It will do you harm. People will think you dissipated if they hear you talk slang; besides it's vulgar, sir; your bye-words ought always to have something medical about them.'

'I beg pardon, sir, I forgot.'

'Well, don't forget again. As I was saying, you buy a small practice; and I should advise you to start in the City. People eat and drink a good deal there, and you will always have patients dropping in who want something for indigestion.'

'Ah! exactly, sir.'

'Well, you give them a little *mistura stomachica,* or you make up a bit of a draught, one-half infusion of *gentian,* the other of *calumba,* with a drachm or two of *compound tincture of cardamoms,* and a few grains of *sodae carb.* This relieves them directly. They are sure to come again, and you get talked of. At last they get fever, and then you are sent for. You know my practice — the pills at night, and the draughts three times a day. You can't do better.'

'No, sir, I know that. And what sort of a house?'

'Ah! why, I can give you a hint or two about that. It should be in a court, if possible, leading out of a thoroughfare. Then you know people needn't be seen when they come to you. Another thing: you should have something to attract attention. I saw a capital idea of this kind the other day. A man has just started (in one of the streets near where I sent you about that bill) with a transparency over his door. It represents a Galen's head and shoulders, with the skin off - an excellent notion; it looks as if the man knew anatomy well; and the figure is holding that — what do you call it? — rod, with a couple of serpents turning round it.'

'A clever contrivance, sir! Splendid!'

'Yes, but it won't do westward, you know. I'll tell you what, too, you should do. Get your diploma put into a nice gilt frame, and hang it up in the ante-room to your shop, beneath the portrait of Dr. Cullen.'

'Yes, sir, that I knew was a good thing; I should have done that, certainly.'

'Well, then you should get married as soon as you can; it shews you to be steady, and women will never employ an unmarried medical man. And, by the way, always contrive to get into their good graces. They are capital advertisements.'

'Advertisements, sir?'

'Yes, they will talk about you, and praise you up. I'll tell you one way of pleasing them — the married ones, at least. Now, if you were asked about diet, what should you say?'

'Enquire what the patient liked best, and let him have it.'

'Nay, that's not exactly the thing. Find out what his wife or his mother would wish to give him, and take care to agree with them. If he has neither the one nor the other, make a point of forbidding what he asks for, and recommend some other article of food instead. Take care, however, that it isn't disagreeable. And as to your manner: treat every complaint made to you seriously; never laugh at hypochondriacal affections; indeed, the less you laugh at all, the better. Keep up your dignity, sir; but be always patient, kind, and conciliatory in your behaviour, especially to women.'

As Mr. Label concluded this piece- of advice, the surgery-door was gently rung by an applicant for relief, who turned out to be a poor woman with a child at the breast, meanly clad, and looking very ill and miserable. 'Well, ma'am, and what's the matter with you?' demanded that gentleman.

'Oh! sir, I've had a hacking cough these three months; it do terrify me so, that I aint had not a wink of sleep for a whole week, and the kernels is come down; and I've got sitch a sore throat that I can't hardly swaller my wittles; and' —

'Hah! let's see — Oh! Mr. Jackson. *Gargarisma commune,* and *haustus ruber, ter die.* The young man will attend to you, ma'am, if you've anything more to say; just look to her, will you, Mr. Jackson; and as to the medicines — n-t-s-n* — you understand.' Mr. Jackson proved that he did, by giving his master a look as nearly akin to a wink, as the distance between them allowed it to be — and Mr. Label went to dinner.

The Apothecary dined early, as he had that evening to exercise his inquisitorial functions at the Hall; previously to doing which, he always found it necessary to refresh his memory. And here we are strongly allured to a 'Digression concerning Examiners,' shewing in what time a man may learn how to ask a hundred questions on any given science, without the labour of previously acquiring the science itself. But we resist temptation. Mr. Label had another reason also for taking his meal betimes; he wished to sip his three glasses of wine after it at leisure, and to sit quietly for an hour or two, which, as he possessed sufficient physiological information to know, would greatly tend to promote digestion.

This agreeable and healthful state of quiescence he was not, however, destined to enjoy. He had scarcely finished his cheese, when the invitation to knock and ring, held out upon the door, was complied with, in a manner which would have frightened any one not professionally accustomed to such disturbances nearly out of his senses. Even Mr. Label was startled; and, before he could regain his composure, the

---

* 'Ne tradantur sine nummo.' 'Don't let them he delivered without the money,' a technical term equivalent to 'No trust.'

servant announced that Mrs. Plummer's carriage was come for him: and that he was expected to go immediately, that lady having been taken suddenly and dangerously ill.

Mrs Plummer was the wife of a rich sugar-baker, and Mr Label had nothing to do for it but to go. Accordingly, he hurriedly adjusted his white neckcloth, pulled down his black velvet waistcoat, which had risen upon his chest in certain transverse folds during his repast, buttoned his brown great coat up to his chin, donned his broad-brimmed beaver, converted his look of ill-humour into an aspect of becoming solemnity, and deposited his person in Mrs Plummer's carriage.

He found the interesting patient (who was of a very jealous disposition) in a state of high nervous excitement, occasioned by an injudicious smile which her husband had bestowed on the pretty housemaid. She was, in fact, in hysterics; and in the height of indulgence in all those elegant and affecting postures, gestures, and workings of the visage, which, as the malady whereof they are the symptoms seldom attacks ladies when they are by themselves, are probably intended by nature to excite pity and commiseration in the minds of the bystanders.

The room having been cleared of all unnecessary persons, and order having been obtained, the lady modulated from a tempest of incoherent vociferations, into a low and pathetic whine; and finally recovered her senses by the means of a smelling-bottle, which she seized with great avidity, in spite of appearing, in other respects, quite unconscious of the presence of surrounding objects.

'Compose yourself, my dear Mrs. P,' said Mr. Label.

'Oh, Mr. Label! Oh, dear! I shall be off again; I'm sure I shall.'

'Don't give way to it, my dear madam. Come, come' (patting her on the back), 'you'll do very well. There, there;

allow me to recommend this little draught; it will do you good, believe me.' So saying, Mr. Label produced from his coat-pocket a small bottle of medicine, of catholic efficacy, which it was his habit to administer on all sudden emergencies. Mrs Plummer gulphed down the potion with as much eagerness as if she had been in danger of perishing from thirst. It was chiefly composed of an aromatic tincture, and very closely resembled a domestic remedy which she frequently had recourse to in private.

'Oh, Mr. Label, I'm such a poor nervous creature!'

'So you are, ma'am; so you are. How is the pulse? Hum — haw! — a hundred; — and the tongue? Ah, I see, a *leetle* feverish. We will take a little febrifuge mixture, and we shall soon get round again, I dare say.'

'Oh! pray don't send me any nasty physic, sir — pray don't; it makes me ill to think of it. I had rather be bled.' Mr. Label ventured to remonstrate.

'I must be bled — I must be bled,' reiterated the lady.

'Plummer will be the death of me; I know he will. Oh, dear! oh, dear! I wish he could know how ill he has made me. Oh, dear! oh, dear! oh, dear!' Here she began to exhibit symptoms of a relapse, which Mr. Label observing, and likewise discovering how (to use a vulgar phrase) the cat jumped, found it useless to contend any longer. He, therefore, did as he was desired; the patient taking due care to faint before an ounce of the vital fluid had been withdrawn from the circulating system.

When the consequences of the operation had subsided, Mr Label made one more effort in behalf of his darling draughts; but he was still unsuccessful, and was obliged to content himself with leaving behind him a couple of pills from a little ivory box, which, as well as the bottle, he made a point of always carrying about with him. Thus disappointed, he next repaired to the Hall. [The list of rejected candidates was of more than usual length on that evening.]

16

THE APOTHECARY

We are sorry that the nature of this work, and our own regard for truth, have prevented us from drawing upon imagination for the above description of the Apothecary. The 'Physician in ordinary to the Masses,' may hereafter become a different kind of personage. When the public shall at length have perceived that the cure of a disorder does not always necessitate the swallowing of physic, they will perhaps adopt some other method of remunerating men than by forcing them to sell drugs at twenty times their real value. The rising generation of practitioners is ripe for the change: let us hope that we may, at no distant period, behold its accomplishment; and that the present system of quackery and deceit will then rank with the by-gone evils of antiquated error, and exploded absurdity.

THE FASHIONABLE PHYSICIAN

He must have killed a great many people to get so rich
MOLIÈRE

THE FASHIONABLE PHYSICIAN

BY R H HORNE

SIR COURTNEY PALMOILE, in the fifty-seventh year of his age, attained the very summit of professional popularity and practice. None of the *haut-ton* could be sick without his advice; no sick personage could die happy without his assistance. In short, there were no bounds to the mental satisfaction and substantial 'relief' which the aristocracy and rich gentry experienced from paying a series of fees to Sir Courtney Palmoile — the most fashionable physician of his day.

With reference to the costume of the class, concerning which we are writing, we have a word to say. Our readers will be pleased to remember that the *ancien regime* of the physician's constant full dress — his black satin smalls, with knee and shoe buckles; his powder, queue, his glass and pin, his point-lace ruffles and wise-headed gold cane — all have fled and evaporated. The character of the courtly physician remains much the same; but the dress is quite altered. The movements and style of manners are also different. They have lost their ball-room effect and presentation; though still very precise, soft, and of feline velvetude in noiseless tread, so that the ear of noble sickness knoweth not of their advance or retirement — 'Come like Palmoile, so depart!' There is a certain something, however, about the hands, and the movements from the elbow to the wrist, of a physician of this class, which has never changed. They are continually displayed in a pacifying, dulcifying, deprecatory, reconciling, soothing, and patting position — of which action and expression the Doctor in Punch is the exact prototype. In place of the ruffles, however, he now wears an ostentatious mourning-ring — the gift of a dear, deceased patient, who died under his hands; and sometimes pearl studs, attached to very large and finely 'got-up' lawn wrist-bands. He always wears flannel down to his very wrists, where you just see it peep. He always wears a superfine great-coat, with long skirts, in the pocket of which he carries a stethoscope. This is a newly-invented instrument to examine the chest; and, in its genuine form, resembles a thick wooden ruler; but, as used by a Fashionable Physician, it commonly appears in the shape of a penny trumpet. He wears long black trousers and short gaiters, and his shoes are generally too large for his feet, in order to admit of extra flannel socks, to keep his toes warm in his carriage during winter. His hair is short and rather straight, but very smooth, so that the peculiar shape of his scientific skull is clearly defined in the outline. After he has been knighted, he is liable to brush his hair up in front, in a high and copious manner, as if the hair was hurraing! This is, however, a rare instance of his imprudent display of feeling, and in almost all cases his head has a sleek appearance. His chariot is of laudanum colour, faintly streaked with cinnamon; or of a profound green mixture, which has a bitter look. His harness is all black, with an occasional stud of silver or bronze; and his liveries are brown drab, or Oxford-grey. His coachman is very thin, and holds a thin black stick of a whip in a highly-precise and formally-useless manner. His horses are disagreeably dark, and in a somewhat jaded condition. They are, however, among the most intelligent of their species; and, as they turn a corner and advance down a long and handsome street, you see their ears work to and fro with evident anxiety whenever there are any houses within sight, the shutters of which are at all closed. On arriving opposite a house where the shutters are closed from top to bottom, their ears fall back with an uncomfortable look of self-consciousness, and they quicken their pace; but where only one floor has the shutters partially closed, their ears shoot out and point to the house, while they slacken their trot, in anticipation of a cheek from the coachman. The footman of this equipage is also very thin: speaks in an under-tone, and has the same expression of face, in answering a question, that you see in an undertaker's clerk or foreman when engaged with a customer. A Fashionable Physician has his portrait painted at full length every third year, by the most fashionable painters among the Royal Academicians, and is represented in a sitting position, at a splendid table, covered with the works of Galen and Hippocrates, upon the top of which are piled several inscribed with his own name in a larger gold letter, while a bust of Esculapius, with an expression of great humility, stands pale before him. The royal artist seldom conveys the characteristic look of a Fashionable Physician, and few pencils are there which could ever succeed in delineating a face so softly advising, so acquiescingly gossiping and prescribing, so fee-thinking and insinuating, and so

20

saturated with legacy-hunting tenderness. How much of this has been represented by the artist of our 'Heads,' we leave the reader to determine. We venture to observe, however, that a more characteristically insincere face we never beheld: while the general action and expression denote the most tender solicitude about his patient's welfare, his half-closed eye seems to be prying into a purse.

Sir Courtney Palmoile was not always the great man above described. His origin was extremely humble. We feel considerable delicacy and hesitation in mentioning the fact that his real name was Grub. We can fancy the recollection might be very humiliating to any creature of the grub genus, after it had become a visiting butterfly, and was habituated to bask in the gold of the noon-tide sun; and pass, on simmering wings, from patient flower to flower. The fact, however, must be recorded. Mr Grub was originally an inhabitant of a small country town, where he followed no particular calling.

But finding, in due course, that a certain official 'calling' was likely to follow him, if he continued to indulge his philosophical indolence any longer, he made up his mind to be a chemist and druggist, and to practise as an apothecary at the same time, in order to assist the sale of his wares. To avoid the loss of time in apprenticeship, as well as the law on the subject, he hired the services of a starving apothecary who had 'passed the Hall,' and placed his name over the door instead of his own.

It has been ascertained by philanthropic legislators, that the highest degree of the healing art should be exclusively devoted to those who can pay highest for the idea of obtaining relief. Various degrees of rank are, therefore, established. The highest rank in medical practice is a Fellow of the College of Physicians. To be eligible to this rank, all the usual gradations of knowledge and experience required in other professions are not only considered unnecessary, but detrimental and damnatory. It is requisite that a man should not have been an apothecary, on pain, we believe, of a heavy fine; nor a surgeon, on pain of a heavier. All that is required is this, the candidate for medical aristocracy must have been 'educated' at Oxford or Cambridge. Now, at neither of these erudite cities is there any public hospital, infirmary, or any institution for clinical practice, which will bear the designation of a medical school; — but they read the Axioms of Hippocrates, which have been long since universally exploded by practitioners. Being rendered competent to take charge of human life by these equivocal studies, the candidates are examined before the Great Authorities, probably without ever having seen a single dissection, nor, possibly, a single case of smallpox, measles, or common fever! The Licentiates of the College of Physicians may have had regular and elaborate education and practice in Scotland, Dublin, or London; but it is only the Oxford and Cambridge gentlemen who can become Fellows — prescribe in letters of gold, and be considered as 'pure' physicians. No base initiatory studies retarded the progress of Sir Courtney's fortune. He managed to take a good shop; he hired the services of one who *had* gone through such studies; he bought a new hat with a broadish brim, and went about advising.

Mr Grub, always polite, simpering, and obsequious, was naturally a rising man. Being also a lucky man, success attended all his movements and designs; and, eventually, the wealthy old widow of a methodistical chiropodist left him a handsome legacy in token of her lasting esteem.

Now rose the night-cap of Mr William Grub, in midnight reverie! Perish for ever the dark memories of early years, the baseborn herbs, the nauseous drugs! The spirit of the Grub burst its narrow confines; he sold his business and went to Oxford.

'The discipline of the English Universities,' said Dr. Macmichael, 'is such as to be, in every sense, a security of the moral character of the candidate(!): by giving him right feelings(!), and enlarging his mind, it is the best security you can possibly have. The circumstance of having completed the residence required by the English Universities, and been subject to the discipline(!) observed there, as attested by the degree(!), is the most obvious and the highest testimonial of character and general education that can be procured. I can conceive of no one better!'

Excellent man! most 'pure physician.' Mr William Grub, after that period of residence, which is, 'in every sense, the best security for moral character,' and has the best security of receiving the divine gift of 'right feelings,' left College as the humble follower of a dashing young blade of rank and fortune, to whom he had rendered himself agreeable by his subserviency. This young gentleman, wishing to make some trifliing change in his not very domestic arrangements, shortly after his arrival in London, informed his follower, without any waste of time in delicate preamble, that he intended to make him take up his abode elsewhere; and accordingly Mr William Grub installed himself in a new house, and changing his name to Palmoile, had it engraved on a brass plate above his knocker. His generous patron next introduced him to a very handsome lady, attired in green velvet, and a hat and feather, who was persuaded to listen to his addresses, and shortly afterwards married him. On the conclusion of the ceremony, the young nobleman slapped the bridegroom on the shoulder, ejaculating, 'Grub, my boy, you're really a very useful, talented sort of fellow — and I'll take care of you.'

His lordship was as good as his word. William Grub, *alias* Palmoile, became a Fashionable Physician. Assisted by this powerful influence, he was soon elected a Fellow of the Royal College of Physicians, — that 'royal road' to 'learning' the science of building a carriage out of tombstones, and filling coffers from the rich mine of human weakness.

Dr. Palmoile now took up his pen; he saw that it was good to be literary, and scribbled away. He saw that Scotchmen always advanced in the world whenever they had a chance. Regretting he was only a Yorkshireman, he did what he could to remedy the deficiency by hiring a Scotchman as a servant. This man was a wit, in his way, and 'ower fond o' the toddy:' so Dr Palmoile used now and then to make him excessively drunk, and, taking down what he said, the Doctor was enabled by these means to concoct an article exactly in the high-vaulting and voluminously verbose style of a notorious professor of Moral Philosophy. These truly astonishing productions found a ready admission into the mimetic pages of a certain London Magazine, where they were much praised by his friends and patients for the redundant fancy and unexceptionable morality they displayed.

Dr. Palmoile now presented to the public his 'great work.' It certainly contained some very valuable matter. This he had discovered in one of the manuscripts of the library of the Royal College of Physicians, and having copied out all he wanted, he watched his opportunity, and burned the original.* This elegant work, in nine volumes royal, was entitled, 'On the Diseases and Disarrangements peculiar to Fashionable Life.' It was dedicated to the higher Circle, by their most humble, affectionate, and obedient servant, the author.

'Doctor, my buck!' — said his young patron — 'Come under my arm to the Drawing Room, and I'll take care of you!' The Doctor was accordingly presented at Court. He laid his fulsome volumes, bound in crimson and gold, at his Majesty's feet and was commanded to 'rise Sir Courtney Palmoile!'

Shortly after attaining this military order, so appropriate to a professor of the 'healing art,' Sir Courtney received the shocking intelligence, while seated at breakfast with his lady, that their friend and patron had been shot in a duel. 'Now,' said the medical knight, replacing his uplifted muffin on the plate, 'I must take care of myself.' The young nobleman lived just long enough to make his will, in which he left the Doctor and his wife, each, an annuity of five hundred pounds per annum. A very pleasant and prosperous time they had.

While he turned gossip into gold, she turned day into night. A profession, the humane purposes of which — in the alleviation of sickness and pain, the eradication of disease, and the endeavour to prolong the duration of human life — are of a character so extensive and so important to the health and happiness of the world; a profession, in the right and qualified exercise of which, the lives of his fellow creatures are placed with humble reliance in the practitioner's hands, ought to be guarded by all the means possible to be devised, against both the uneducated and ill-educated, whatever degree of rank and assumption they may claim and possess in the dazzling glare of fashion and notoriety. But guarded it is not: on the contrary, great facilities are given to the ingress of imposters, and these *facilities* are guarded and preserved with the most watchful solicitude. We have only space to give a few memoranda of certain highly patronised

---

*This was a trifle. Sir Everard Home, after publishing his own works, in which he made what use he pleased of the unpublished manuscripts of John Hunter, deposited in the College of Surgeons, thought proper to burn them all. The act betrayed itself, for he set fire to his house in doing it, the quantity being so great. - See a masterly and comprehensive article on 'Medical Reform,' in No. VII, of 'The London and Westminster Review.'

proceedings, which may not, however, be altogether without instruction.

A Fashionable Physician has a favourite disease, and a favourite remedy — each of which changes like any other fashion. Sometimes it is the liver — then the lungs — then the head — then the stomach — sometimes even the heart. The stomach, however, is the favourite that 'comes round' the oftenest. This is a *corps de reserve* for all failures, and a prescription for it must generally do good; because, while poor people are ill from a deficiency of food, and frequently from taking ardent spirits instead, the rich people are mostly ill from intemperance in all things.

A Fashionable Physician always leaves town directly after the 'season,' and his patients *keep* till his return. Those, however, who do not remain behind, are advised to betake themselves to the very place where he is going. But, among those who stay in town, there is seldom a cessation of fees, because a physician of this class employs several less fortunate physicians to call for him, he allowing them a 'certain something' upon the fees handed over to him. Under their inferior skill, the patients are sometimes actually getting quite well; but, at this dangerous crisis, the 'great man' suddenly returns to town, and, strange to say, the whole of them are again taken ill, as if seized by an epidemic.

We once heard of a physician who, being on his promotion, and very anxious to elevate himself into fashionable practice, always called himself Dr G——, Perpetual President Extraordinary of the Royal and National Eye Institution. As nobody had ever heard of this most excellent, majestic, and extensive Eye Institution, it was natural that its perpetual President Extraordinary should some time or other be questioned on the subject. 'Pray, Doctor, where in the world *is* this extraordinary Eye Institution?' Drawing himself up, he replied, '*I* am the Institution!'

A Fashionable Physician seldom loses the sense of his own dignity, through any inadvertent act of private good feeling. He would see any friend die before him rather than condescend to bleed him with his own hand — for that is expressly the business of a mere surgeon — and these kinds of things are never to be thought of for a moment by a 'pure physician!'

IN SICKNESS AND IN HEALTH

A consultation of Fashionable Physicians recently took place on the case of an elderly and very amiable lady of rank, who was undoubtedly dying. Sir Courtney Palmoile had attended her from the commencement; and when he saw that nothing more could be done, he very properly called in the assistance of the celebrated Dr Aymen Toom, LSD, FEE; and Sir William Sganarelle, a descendant from the famous French physician of that name, who flourished in the time of the historian Moliere. They were shown into a large room at the end of a suite; and, while passing through, a little nephew of the dying lady, spurred by a sudden curiosity to overhear the wonderful secrets and discourse of these profound magicians, slipped in at a private door, and squeezed himself behind a tall bookcase that stood at the farther end. The three professors of elegant medicine entered — carefully closed the door — divested themselves of their hats and great coats, and drawing close to the fire a small, refreshment table, on which some wine, cake, and hot-house grapes were placed, began to rub and toast their knees, and take something to sustain nature and strengthen them for the consultation.

'When we look at the case in all its bearings,' said Sir William Sganarelle, drawing a newspaper from his pocket, 'and analyse the various thoughts and feelings caned into complex activity upon the occasion, how plain it was to foresee that the mutual exactions superinduced thereby, would infallibly occasion the separation of Madame Grisi from her husband. This is a very excellent plum cake, isn't it?'

'Excellent,' said Sir Courtney Palmoile: 'but it's my opinion, with great deference to you, Sir William, that this separation is likely to be feigned, from policy. They both see that her reputation here is at stake. She dare not seem to sanction her husband's conduct. To think of the impertinence of a singing woman's husband actually calling out a member of the Royal College of — I mean of the British Aristocracy, merely on account of a sort of overture of passing gallantry, to which her position in this country naturally subjected her! If such audacious resentments are to be tolerated for a moment, what in the world will become of the respect due to hereditary legislation? Shocking!"

'I wish,' said Dr Aymen Toom, with a profound look — 'I wish, for the sake of example and a great moral lesson, that they had shot each other.'

THE FASHIONABLE PHYSICIAN

'And that they should have lingered for a period of fifty fees,' interposed Sir Courtney, smiling with diplomatic humour. Whereat the other two rubbed their knees, and manifested sensations of additional comfort and self-complacency.

They now talked of Lord Durham; and blamed him for every thing he had offered to do; for everything he had done; for all his past political life; and for everything he might do in future. They agreed that the Radicals were a precious set — that the Whigs were a precious set — and then they laughed at the Tories. They entered seriously into the consequences of Biddle's prospective banking system in America — into the merits of the King of Oude's sauce — of L E Ude's ditto — and of Sir George Smart's last composition. They now insinuated a tacit understanding of drinking the health of the President of the College of Physicians — they applauded the Duke of Wellington — they touched upon 'The Quarterly Review' — they criticised the Queen's horsemanship — and passed some capital jokes upon Louis Phlippe's sister.

While they were all laughing in full glee at Sir Courtney's finishing touch of rather high-flavoured wit, the tall bookcase was seen to rock, and then lean forward! The next instant, down came the whole concern flat on the floor; and amidst the chaos of gilt-edged volumes and rising dust stood the crinched-up figure of the little imp of a nephew, with stiff-spread fingers, open mouth, and round, staring eyes!

Before they could recover the shock, or at all understand the dreadful scene, the door opened, and a footman entered with the patient's compliments, informing them, that 'in consequence of the great relief she had experienced by a touch of the lancet from a common doctor, a brother of her nephew's private tutor, who had accidentally called, she was now seated in her dressing-gown by the fire, taking a cup of tea.' She had also desired the servant to say, 'that although this obscure doctor had only been educated in the Edinburgh and London universities, he was evidently a most skilful and honourable practitioner, and she had, therefore, great pleasure in recommending him to their kind patronage and assistance.'

27

THE MEDICAL STUDENT

We murder to dissect (!)
WORDSWORTH

THE MEDICAL STUDENT

BY PAUL PRENDERGAST

ENTER abruptly on the scene — (the lobby of the Anatomical Theatre, _____ Hospital) — the subject of our present sketch: a young gentleman, of about five feet eight inches in height, with dull darkish eyes, and eyebrows to match — interlacing over the root of the nose, the last-mentioned feature being large, long, and fleshy, and in excellent keeping with a couple of thick projecting lips. The complexion is a kind of smoky tallow; the forehead is narrow and sloping, but the contour of the rest of the head is concealed by a four-and-ninepenny gossamer, with a very narrow brim and sundry indentations in front, worn sideways in the most approved fashion of billiard-room frequenters and visitors of night-houses. A black neckerchief tied à la *Ben Brace,* a very high and not very clean shirt-collar, a rough Flushing jacket garnished with broad black bone buttons, a very long waistcoat of a shawl pattern, and blue shaggy trousers splashed with mud at their terminations, complete the costume. The tout-ensemble forms an illustration of 'December fashions for Gentlemen,' as modified in the person of a probationary guardian of the public health 'in statu pupillari,' — that is, in the course of 'walking the Hospitals;' a species of discipline which is strongly analogous to what is termed in some establishments for the reformation of offenders, 'unproductive labour.' The parallel, indeed, between this system and that pursued at a certain Institution in the suburban retirement of Brixton, is remarkably close, as regards the advantages of each, both to the individual and to society. The hands of this member of the 'HEADS OF THE PEOPLE' (and tails of his profession) are lodged in the wide pockets appertaining to his hirsute outer garment; and under the left arm is carried a greasy octavo volume, the lids of which have been marbled in the process of binding, and stained in the pursuit of knowledge. But it is time that our head (like Friar Bacon's, 't is a brazen one) should speak.

'VA-RIE-TY! — Hallo! Bill, how did you get home last night? You're looking seedy this morning, you are; but what made you bolt so soon? You should have stopped, man, and heard 'The Little Pigs;' it was given in regular bang-up style, I can tell you — uncommon gentlemanly chap the bass singer, when you come to know him — came out afterwards in 'The Wolf;' my eye! what a voice he has; shouldn't I like to walk into his *larynx*! Then there was that little girl with the blue bonnet and white feathers — you know, Bill — eh? — she flared-up like bricks in 'The last rose of Summer.' Well, after that, Jim and I felt rather queer, so we had a Welsh rabbit, a pint of stout a-piece, and two goes of whiskey; and here I am this morning, as fresh as a daisy, my tulip! I think I want some stimulus though. Come, I say, what'll you have; let's send to Billy Baxlow's for some half-and-half — I'll toss you for it, if you like. Have a cigar? Deuced pretty girl where I bought 'em — promised to go with me to 'The Eagle' to-morrow — that's the ticket, an't it? Why, there goes nine! Shan't you go in to demonstration; Slogo gives the 'Reflections of the Peritoneum' this morning, and I've got an *abdomen* in: not one of the branches of the *cœliac* have I made out yet, and the 'stiff 'un 's' to be turned to-morrow. Come along.' — (Exeunt Arcades.)

In a large circular theatre, covered with a dome, and surrounded for one-third of its height (excepting the small space required for the performance) by benches rising one above the other on an inclined plane, are seated an audience of about two hundred, presenting a great variety both as to physiognomy and costume. Opposite to them stands a large table covered with a linen cloth, from beneath which a pair of legs and arms are seen protruding. Behind the table there hangs a board, whereon are displayed telegraphed illustrations of divers interesting peculiarities in the human frame. On one side of this piece of scenery a skeleton dangles from a kind of single-posted gibbet; on the other there is a door for the entrance of the lecturer. A gallery runs round the upper part of the Theatre, and the whole is surmounted by a skylight in the dome. A confused hum of voices arises from the medical multitude, some of whom are engaged in earnest, some in facetious conversation; some in copying the diagrams, others in paring their nails; while others again are arranging their note-books and cutting their lead pencils, and one or two are pelting each other with pellets of chewed paper. It is just lecture-time, and public expectation, strained to its highest pitch, is frequently disappointed by the entrance of some studious young man, anxious for a seat in the front row, to gain which he is obliged to creep under the table. On each of these occasions, the individual who thus becomes unfortunately conspicuous is saluted with a round of applause, followed by a general cachinnation.

The lecturer now makes his appearance, and, after the necessary hushing and hemming has subsided, commences his discourse. He has proceeded for about five minutes — a scampering up the stairs is heard — the gallery door slams violently. The cause of this disturbance, namely, Mr Thomas Hogmore, our hero, enters, and encounters a glance of reproof from the interrupted and angry lecturer. This he sustains with a visage of great gravity, which, the moment the stare is withdrawn, he exchanges for a peculiar grimace, formed by thrusting the tongue into the cheek, and momentarily closing the left eye. He then sits down, composing himself in an attitude of attention; his legs being supported against the iron railing, and his fore-teeth resting on the knobbed extremity of his thick stick.

At this period the board of diagrams is lowered, for the purpose of exhibiting one of them more clearly to the class. The effect of this movement is to produce a universal peal of laughter. The marble bust of a late celebrated teacher of anatomy, which had been before concealed, is now exposed to view, embellished by the ingenious Mr. Hogmore (previously to the lecture) with a pair of moustachios and an imperial, cut out of black cloth, and stuck on with gum. The lecturer stands astonished for a moment at this unexpeted merriment; but, on turning round, at once discovers its cause.

'Gentlemen — some — I may say — individual, has thought proper to disgrace himself!' [Bravo! Hear, hear!] 'Gentlemen, whoever that individual is, I may venture to affirm that he ought to be ashamed of himself — I need say no more. I throw myself on the good sense and gentlemanly feeling of the class.' [Hear, hear! Shame! Turn him out!] in which shouts the culprit loudly joins.

After this occurence, the lecture proceeds, but having been prolonged a little beyond the hour; its termination is hastened by a general scraping of feet, and a fit of coughing which suddenly seizes the class. We will now accompany our neophyte, trusting, that he may have been duly edifid by what he has heard, to his four o'clock dinner at that species of restaurateur's, which obtains, in his own classic vocabulary, the epithet of slap-bang.

'Now, then, Jack, my boy, what are you going to tackle? I've been hard at work all the morning with the *abdominal aorte,* and I shall be regularly knocked up if I don't pitch in pretty smartish; here, Sally, what have you got?'

'Boiled beef, Sir, and greens — well done; roast veal and 'am — good cut; haricot mutton; liver and bacon; calf's head and brains — just up — I can recommend that, Sir; hashed venison' (with peculiar emphasis); 'chops and steaks.'

'Ah! let's have some liver and bacon. By the way Jack, are you to give the minute anatomy of the liver at the College?'

'I don't know; I hope not.'

'So do I. Mine was a capital one this morning.'

'Yes. Why didn't you have it injected?'

'Too much of a fork out; besides, you can cram the liver from *plates.*'

With this kind of conversation the rest of the meal is sweetened. At its conclusion :—

'Sally,' (cries Mr. Hogmore), 'what's the damage?'

'One calf's liver and bacon, Sir, ten — potatoes, eleven — one bread, twelve — two stouts, one and nine — a Stilton, one and eleven — and celery, I think you had, Sir.'

'Yes.'

'Two and a penny, Sir, if you please.'

'Oh! two bob and a brown is it? I say, Sally, I wish I had lots of tin, for your sake.'

'Do you, Sir? Hem!'

'Yes. I say, where do you walk on Sundays?'

'Sometimes at one place, sometimes at another. *(apart)* — Coming, Sir, directly.'

'No, but come, don't mizzle: I've something to say to you.'

'Well, what is it?'

'I say, Sally, you're a very pretty girl.'

'Oh! don't be a stupid — there now look at my foot — see what you've done.'

32

Here it must be observed, that Mr. Hogmore, in order to give due effect to his last complimentary speech, treads engagingly on the young lady's foot; leaving thereby the muddy impression of a double row of small nails on the delicately turned instep. Having achieved this act of gallantry, he puts down the reckoning and sallies forth to 'wander at his own sweet will' down Fleet Street, or the Strand, smoking a bad cigar, and jostling the passengers as he walks along.

His time is thus occupied till he goes to the evening lecture, after which he returns to his third floor lodging to receive a party of friends, who meet to amuse themselves with a game at whist. This sort of employment is generally called spending time; in the present instance, however, a laudable economy of that article is displayed — a practical contradiction being given to the vulgar adage asserting the impossibility of doing two things at once. The attention of the players is divided between their game and their hot whiskey and water, a tumbler of which accompanies the heap of counters by the side of each individual. The contents of the glasses are renewed, from time to time, from a green bottle on the table, and a kettle which sings away on the fire; and which, in the course of the evening, is twice replenished from the wash-hand-stand in the adjoining bed-room. Between the play and potation, the spirits of the company become elevated to a very lofty pitch; the exhausted source of the aqueous supply, an its empty receptacle, are anathematised in the vernacular form, the candlesticks are flung into the grate, and a general 'sortie' is made in quest of adventures. The young gentlemen 'jump Jim Crow' in the street, to the music of their own voices, wrench off knockers and bell-handles, shout, yell, assault a policeman, are finally consigned to the station-house, and discharged the next morning on payment of the usual fine for inebriety.

We will now imagine that having happened to receive an invitation from some gentleman with whom his family are acquainted, our hero has made the requisite alterations (or what he considers such) in his exterior, and is sitting at table in decent society.

The master of the house is decapitating a hare. His guest remarks :—

Ah! you're hung up, rather, Sir, I think; you've got hold of the *ligamentum nuchæ*; it's very big and strong in some animals — I made it out the other day in a N——r — he was pretty well off for one.'

'Made it out, Sir,' asks a gentleman sitting opposite, 'how?'

A nudge from his next neighbour reminds him of the presence of ladies. Instead, therefore, of conveying his meaning in words, he looks significantly around on the company, and bestowing a wink of much expression on his interrogator, holds his knife and fork like a couple of pens, severs, as if by some sleight-of-hand the fat from the lean of a piece of meat on his plate, winks again on the querist, and applies himself to the discussion of the viands with renewed assiduity.

He is asked to take wine: — 'Most happy,' he replies, and familiarly invites a gentleman, some forty years his senior, to join him. On a similar honour being done him by his host, his answer is,

'Thank'ee, Sir, I've got some.'

The cloth is now removed, and dessert introduced. A young clergyman present happens to be speaking of the place which he took in the classical tripos at Cambridge. 'Oh! you've been up, then?' says our hero. 'What sort of an examination did they give you? Did they behave like gentlemen, or bully you at all?' A civil reply is given to his question, and he proceeds :— 'However, your examination is nothing to ours; I've been grinding these three months, and Hoaxley tells me I shan't be fit for three more; I'm well up in anatomy too, and none of 'em know much about *that* at the Hall. But that's the very reason they work a man so. Why you're only examined in Latin and Greek; and we have Latin, and the Lord knows what besides. I've passed my Latin examination, that's one good job: they gave me a whole page, and if I hadn't looked over the fellow next me I think I should have been floored. I hate Latin — what's the use of it? As if Latin would teach you to take up the *femoral artery* — parcel of humbug!'

'You are fond of poetry, I suppose, Mr. Hogmore,' enquires a young lady, trotting the orator out.

'Poetry? — eh? — what? — oh! — I haven't learnt any since I left school. I used to like the short verses best. Ha! ha! ha!'

'You like music, then, I am sure.'

'Music? Oh! I like a jolly good song. Did you ever hear 'The Sea?''

'No, I have not had that pleasure; is it pretty?'

'Just isn't it? Nor 'The Bay of Biscay?''

'No.'

'Ah! then, I'd just advise you to go to 'The Coal Hole' — no — that is — I mean — you can't do that exactly — but those are the kind of songs I like.'

'The Coal Hole! Dear me, what an odd place to sing in. How very amusing!'

'I should think,' remarks the wit of the party, 'that it would be an admirable scene for the performance of 'La Cenerentola."

This sally occasions a general merriment, which Mr. Hogmore conceives to be furnished at his expense, and accordingly regards the speaker with a look of anything but complacency; muttering, at the same time, the word 'personal,' as if he considered the title of Rossini's opera capable of bearing that construction.

'What do you think of Phrenology?' demands a maiden of thirty, in a cerulean dress, with a disposition conformable.

'What all that stuff about the bumps? — all my eye — regular sell — won't go down at our place; as if the *mastoid process* was the organ of Murder!'

'That, I suppose, Mr. Hogmore,' says an intellectual looking, middle-aged man, with a capacious forehead and penetrating eyes, 'is one of the facts of Phrenology, according to your teachers?'

'Yes. I'll trouble you for some of those walnuts.'

'Well, but what do they tell you then is the use of the brain?'

'Oh! we're not examined in that. It's the great centre of the nervous system.'

'Did not Gall and Spurzheim, Sir, prosecute their enquiries according to Inductive Philosophy?'

'Oh! I don't know. Philosophy's all moonshine. I like something practical. By the way, I'll tell you a capital joke. Gall had a son; the young chap had the bump of self-approbation too big; so old Gall got a tin plate, and a screw fixed to the head with an apparatus that he invented, and screwed the plate tighter and tighter every day to keep down the bad bump.'

'Indeed; and pray with what result?'

'Child kicked the bucket — hopped the twig — went off in convulsions! Ha, ha, ha, ha, ha!'

'Is not that story rather apocryphal?'

'Apoc— eh? It was Gall or Spurzheim, I forget which.'

35

The ladies retire; the gentlemen talk about horses, politics, agriculture, and practical meteorology, the state of oats, and of the weather, until coffee is announced.

Music is the order of the evening: a lady sits down to the piano, to take a part in 'La ci darem' la mano,' in the middle of which our young gentleman signalises himself by a sudden and loud ebullition of mirth, probably imagining that he is listening to a comic song.

The music not suiting his taste, he betakes himself into a corner, and soon becomes engaged in deep and earnest conversation with a medical friend who has accompanied him. His remarks are quite audible :—

'Well, I never thought that was the kick, however. Why, they gave us wine and water after dinner, in great glass jugs — without sugar too! I'd rather have had some 'cold without.''

'What do you think of the girl who is singing?' asks his friend.

'Oh! she's smartish — deuced fine neck — *clavicles* and *sterno-cleido-mastoidei* too prominent though. *Crico-arytenoidei postici* and *laterales* very well developed, I fancy, judging from her voice. Talking of that, I wish you'd give us a grind — ask us anything?'

'Well then, come, what have you between the layers of the great *omentum*?'

'What have you? — come, no gammon! — why nothing to be sure.'

'Oh! haven't you though? I can tell you they rejected Popjoy on that very question last Thursday.'

'What did they want him to say then?'

'Why, *halitus* to be sure.'

'Pooh! that's a regular catch question. I tell you what — if they floor me on a question like that, I'll pretty soon floor them, that's all. But, I say, they're going; come, let's be off; I'm tired — arn't you? — we shall be just in time for 'The Cyder Cellars,' and I'm tarnation hungry.' — (Exeunt.)

We shall conclude with a brief summary of Mr. Hogmore's remaining moral and intellectual qualities.

The leading feature of his disposition is *amour propre*.He piques himself greatly on his sharpness and cunning, and, considering every one else a rogue, is especially solicitous to avoid being taken in or deceived. Accordingly, his favourite maxim is not merely to doubt, but positively to disbelieve whatever he does not clearly understand. His convictions, however firm, are, consequently, of a very limited nature. History is with him little more than a 'grand peut-être,' and he probably esteems the account of Julius Caesar's death quite as apocryphal as the story of St George and the Dragon: as he believes nothing but what he can comprehend, so he comprehends nothing that he cannot see. Anatomy is, in his estimation, the most exalted of all sciences, and this not in consequence of its real bearings upon medicine — for of those he has very little idea; but because there is something in the mechanical process by which a knowledge of the human frame is acquired, particularly gratifying to his taste and genius. Refinement is, in his opinion synonymous with effeminacy, and he is perfectly innocent of the fine arts in general, and of literature in particular. To the latter, indeed, he seems to have a conscientious objection, as though it tended to interfere with his professional pursuits. He thinks it much better to employ his leisure hours in drinking, smoking, playing practical jokes, and investigating human nature wherever it may be seen to the least advantage. His studies are of a material, his pleasures of an animal nature.

It is not denied that there are exceptions to the above description of a Medical Student. There are those who have adopted their profession as a branch of science, and a means of benefiting mankind. In the revolting tasks which unavoidably fall to their lot, they engage not from inclination, but from duty: these are Philosophers, and so many as there are of them, so many gentlemen are there in the Medical Profession.

THE MONTHLY NURSE

From the very moment the mistress of the house is brought to bed, every female in it, from my lady's gentlewoman to the cinder-wench, becomes an inch taller for it.

TRISTRAM SHANDY

THE MONTHLY NURSE

BY LEIGH HUNT

THE MONTHLY NURSE — taking the class in the lump, without such exceptions as will be noticed before we conclude — is a middle-aged, motherly sort of a gossiping, hushing, flattering, dictatorial, knowing, ignorant, not very delicate, comfortable, uneasy, slip-slop kind of a blinking individual, between asleep and awake, whose business it is — under Providence and the doctor — to see that a child be not ushered with too little officiousness into the world, nor brought up with too much good sense during the first month of its existence. All grown people, with her, (excepting her own family), consist of wives who are brought to bed, and husbands who are bound to be extremely sensible of the supremacy of that event; and all the rising generation are infants in laced caps, not five weeks old, with incessant thirst, screaming faces, thumpable backs, and red little minnikin hands tipped with hints of nails. She is the only maker of caudle in the world. She takes snuff ostentatiously, drams advisedly, tea incessantly, advice indignantly, a nap when she can get it, cold whenever there is a crick in the door, and the remainder of whatsoever her mistress leaves to eat or drink, provided it is what somebody else would like to have. But she drinks rather than eats. She has not the relish for a 'bit o' dinner' that the servant-maid has; though nobody but the washerwoman beats her at a 'dish o' tea,' or at that which 'keeps cold out of the stomach,' and puts weakness into it. If she is thin, she is generally straight as a stick, being of a condition of body that not even drams will tumefy. If she is fat, she is one of the fubsiest of the cosy; though rheumatic withal, and requiring a complexional good-nature to settle the irritabilities of her position, and turn the balance in favour of comfort or hope. She is the victim of watching; the arbitress of her superiors; the servant, yet rival, of doctors; the opposer of innovations; the regretter of all old household religions as to pap-boats, cradles, and swathes; the inhabitant of a hundred bedrooms; the Juno Lucina of the ancients, or goddess of child-birth, in the likeness of a cook-maid. Her greatest consolation under a death (next to the corner-cupboard, and the not having had her advice taken about a piece of flannel) is the handsomeness of the corpse; and her greatest pleasure in life, is when lady and baby are both gone to sleep, the fire bright, the kettle boiling, and her corns quiescent. She then first takes a pinch of snuff, by way of pungent anticipation of bliss, or as a sort of concentrated essence of satisfaction; then a glass of spirits — then puts the water in the tea-pot — then takes another glass of spirits (the last having been a small one, and the coming tea affording a 'counteraction') — then smoothes down her apron, adjusts herself in her arm-chair, pours out the first cup of tea, and sits for a minute or two staring at the fire, with the solid complacency of an owl, — perhaps not without something of his snore, between wheeze and snuff-box.

Good and ill-nature, as in the case of every one else, make the great difference between the endurability, or otherwise, of this personage in your house; and the same qualities, in the master and mistress, together with the amount of their good sense, or the want of it, have a like re-action. The good or ill, therefore, that is here said of the class in general, becomes applicable to the individual accordingly. But as all people will get what power they can, the pleasant by pleasant means, and the unpleasant by the reverse, so the office of the Monthly Nurse, be her temper and nature what it will, is one that emphatically exposes her to temptation that way; and her first endeavour, when she comes into a house, is to see how far she can establish an undisputed authority on all points. In proportion to her success or otherwise in this object, she looks upon the lady as a charming, reasonable, fine, weak, cheatable creature, whose husband (as she tells him) 'can never be too grateful for her bearing such troubles on his account;' or as a Frenchified conceited madam, who will turn out a deplorable match for the poor gentleman, and assuredly be the death of the baby with her tantrums about 'natural living,' and her blasphemies against rum, pieces of fat, and Daffy's Elixir. The gentleman in like manner — or 'master,' as the humbler ones call him — is, according as he behaves himself, and receives her revelations for gospel, a 'sweet good man' — 'quite a gentleman' — 'just the very model of a husband for mistress,' &c &c; or, on the other hand, he is a 'very strange gentleman' — 'quite an oddity' one that is 'not to be taught his own good' — that will 'neither be led nor *druv*' — that will 'be the death of mistress with his constant *fidge-fidge* in and out of the room' — and

40

his making her 'laugh in that dreadful manner,' and so forth; — and, as to his 'pretending to hold the baby, it is like a cow with a candlestick.'

'Holding the baby,' indeed, is a science, which she reckons to belong exclusively to herself; she makes it the greatest favour to visitor or servant to let them venture upon a trial of it; and affable intimations are given to the oldest mothers of families, who come to see her mistress, how they will do well to receive a little instruction on that head, and not venture to substitute their fine-spun theories for her solid practice; for your Monthly Nurse (next to a positive grandson) is the greatest teacher of your grandmother how to suck eggs, in the world; and you may have been forty years in the habit of sticking a pin, and find your competency come to nothing before the explanatory pity of her information.

Respecting the 'doctor,' her thoughts cannot be so bold or even so patronising. She is confessedly second to him, while he is present; and when he has left the room, a spell remains upon her from his superior knowledge. Yet she has her hearty likes or dislikes of him too, and on the same grounds of self-reference. If she likes him, there 'never *was* such a beautiful doctor,' except perhaps Sir William, or Doctor Buttermouth (both dead), and always excepting the one that recommended herself. He is a 'fine man' — so patient — so without pride — and yet 'so firm, like;' — nobody comes near him for a difficult case — for a fever case — for the management of a 'violent lady.' If she dislikes him, he is 'queer' — 'odd' — 'stubborn' — has the 'new ways,' — very proper, she has no doubt, but not what she has been used to, or seen practised by the doctors about court. And whether she likes him or not, she has always a saving grace for herself, of superiority to all other nurses, in point of experience and good luck. She has always seen a case of more difficulty than the one in hand, and knows what was done for it; and Doctor Gripps, who is 'always' called in to such cases, and who is a very pleasant though rough sort of gentleman, calls her his 'other right hand,' and 'the *jewel* that rhymes to *gruel.*'

Armed with these potential notions in general, and the strongest possible sense of her vice-royalty over master and mistress for the time being, she takes possession of the new room and the new faces; and the motto of her reign — the *Dieu et Mon Droit* of her escutcheon —

is 'During the month.' This phrase she has always at hand, like a sceptre, wherewith to assert her privileges, and put down objection. 'During the month,' the lady is not to read a book. 'During the month,' nobody is to lay a finger on the bed for the purpose of making it, till her decree goes forth. 'During the month,' the muffle of the knocker is at her disposal. And 'During the month,' the husband is to be nobody, except as far as she thinks fit, not even (for the first week or so) to his putting his head in at the door. You would take him to be the last man who had had anything to do with the business. However, for her own sake, she generally contrives to condescend to become friends with him, and he is then received into high favour — is invited to tea with his wife, at some 'unusually early' period; and Nurse makes a bit of buttered toast for 'master' with her own hand, and not only repeats that 'baby is as like him as two peas' (which it always is, the moment it is born, if the lady's inclination is supposed to set that way), but tells him that she fears he is 'a sad charming gentleman,' for that 'mistress talks of him in her sleep.' The phrases commonest in her mouth are mostly of an endearing or flattering sort, with an implication, in the tone, of her right to bestow them; and she is very aristocratic in her ideas. She tells the lady in her hour of trial, as the highest encouragement to fortitude she can think of, that 'the Queen must suffer the same;' and the babies are always kings and queens, loves, darlings, jewels, and poppets. Beauties also, be sure — and as all babies are beautiful, and the last always more beautiful than the one before it, and 'the child is father to the man,' mankind, according to Nurse, ought to be nothing but a multitude of Venuses and Adonises; aldermen should be mere Cupids full grown; and the passengers in Fleet Street, male and female, slay one another, as they go, with the unbearableness of their respective charms. But she has also modes of speech, simply pathetic or judicious. If the lady, when her health is enquired after, is in low spirits, she is described as 'taking *on so*;' if doing well, it must not be too well, for the honour of the importance of the case, and the general dignity of ailment; and hence the famous answer, 'as well as can be expected.' By the time the baby arrives at the robustness of a fortnight old, and appears to begin to smack its lips, it is manifestly the most ill-used of infant elegancies, if a series of random hits are not made at its mouth and cheeks with a piece of the fat of pig; and, when it is sleepy and yet will 'not go to sleep' (which is a phenomenon usually developed about the time that Nurse wants her tea), or when it is 'fractious' for not having had *enough* pig, or from something else which has been counteracted, or anything but the sly sup of gin lately given it, or the pin which is now running into its back, it is equally clear, that if Daffy, or Godfrey, or rocking the chair, will not do, a perpetual thumping of the back, and jolting of its very soul out, will; and, accordingly, there lies the future lord or lady of the creation, prostrate across the nurse's knees, a lump in a laced cap and interminable clothes, getting redder and redder in the face, ejaculating such agonies between grunt and shout as each simultaneous thump will permit, and secretly saluted by its holder with 'brats,' and 'drat it,' and 'was there ever such an 'obstropulous' little devil!' while her lips are loud in deprecation of the 'naughty milk,' or the 'naughty cot' (which is to be beaten for its ill-behaviour); and 'Dordie' (Georgy) is told to 'go' to a mysterious place, called 'Bye-Bye;' or the whole catechism of nursery interrogation is gone through, from the past tenses of the amenities of 'Was it a poppet then?' and 'Did it break its pretty heart?' up to the future glories of 'Shall it be a King then?' 'Shall it be a King Pepin?' 'Shall it be a Princy-wincy?' a 'Countess?' A 'Duchess?' 'Shall it break the fine gentlemen's hearts with those beautiful blue eyes?' In the midst of tragicomic burlesque of this sort, have risen upon the world its future Marses and Apollos, its Napoleons, its Platos, and its Shakspeares.

Alas! that it should be made a question (ridiculed indeed by the shallow, the nurse among them, but very seriously mooted by philosophers) whether in that first and tenderest month of existence, the little bundle of already made organs, sensations, and passions, does not receive impressions from this frivolous elderly 'nobody,' which may affect the temper and disposition of the future man or woman! whether the 'beautiful fury' — though we confess we never saw such a phenomenon — whether the crash in the china closet, or the sacrifice of a daughter's happiness to a father's will and obstinacy, had not its first seeds sown in the lap of this poppet-dandling simpleton. Not its 'first,' we apprehend. Those, we take it, are of far earlier origin, the little creature being much older than is generally supposed, when it comes under the influence of this its third, and most transitory, and not always most foolish modifier. But we have no doubt that she con-tributes her portion of effect. This is, however, what she herself can by no means comprehend. 'As if any treatment' (she thinks) 'except in the article of rum and sugar, and the mode of holding, can be of conse-quence to one so young!' She is nevertheless very diligent in looking for 'marks' about its body, and tracing them to influences on the mother's mind; and yet she cannot see that the then impressible little creature is still impressible. Heaven and earth are to come together if the piece of fat is not supplied, or the clothes are not of the proper fashion: but the sudden affrightment, the secret blow, the deadening jolt to sleep, or the giving way to nothing but the last rage, these are to be of no importance. She has no doubt, nevertheless, that its brothers and sisters are all impressible, whatever the infant may be; and accordingly, with her usual instinct of the love of power, she generally contrives to do as much inconsiderate harm to them as possible, and lays the seeds of jealousy in their minds - if none be there already - by telling them that they must now cease to look upon themselves as the only important persons in the family, for that 'a little stranger has come to put their noses out of joint.' Pleasing and picturesque intro-duction to the fraternal affections!

Do not despise her; no, not even when pourtrayed as in our artist's picture, under her worst aspect, for a warning. Engage not such a nurse as that if you can help it; yet pity while you refuse her, for perhaps she would not have had that aspect, but for the unnatural sleeplessness to which her duties forced her, nor have been given to that poison by her side, but for some aggravation of care occasioned by domestic troubles of her own. Even she — even that wretched inconti-nent face and burly person — has once been an infant, as we all have, — perhaps flattered for her beauty, (who would now think it?) the darling and the spoil of some weak mother like herself. Thus are errors propagated, till we discover that personal reproach and satire are of little use, and that it is systems which are to be better taught, before individuals can improve. Poor old nurse! Strange indeed would it be to begin with reprobating her! Let us see that she does as little harm as may be, crown (or *half*-crown) her with fees for her caudle, and dismiss her as fast as possible, with a deprecation of her sciatica.

THE MONTHLY NURSE

There is not only a good as well as a bad side in everything (and with the addition of a little good sense to good-nature, you may make a very pleasant nurse even out of such an one as we have described), but there are exceptions in all classes, better even than mere partakers of bad and good. The Monthly Nurse, as you ascend in society, is not seldom a highly respectable woman, who is nearly all that she should be — mild, firm, and well-meaning; and we have known instances — or rather we should say, as far as our personal knowledge is concerned, one rare instance — in which the requisite qualifications were completed, and the precious individual (for when can a mother's luck be greater?) was an intelligent gentlewoman! This is what the assistant — moulder of the first month of the existence of a human being ought always to be, and what she always *would be,* if the world itself were older, and every the humblest and earliest form of education regarded as the important and sacred thing which it is.

The poets, who are the vindicators of beautiful and everlasting truths, in contradistinction to the fleeting deformities of mistakes and half-truths, made the greatest goddesses of antiquity preside over childbirth; and the reader, supposing him to be the worthy reader of whatsoever relates to humanity, and what small and indifferent things are its least dignified infirmities compared with its powers and affections, will not be sorry to have any ill-taste taken out of the mouth of his imagination on this subject by a passage from one of the earliest of them — supposed by some to have been Homer himself — in which the glorious old Greek, whoever he was, celebrates the birth of Apollo, and makes heaven and earth, the goddesses, the trees, the green meadows, and the incarnation of the spirit of sunshine, contribute to render it beautiful. We quote the version of Mr Elton, as better even than Chapman's, only wishing that he had said 'prevailing,' or some more potent word of that sort, instead of 'valiant,' as the latter has come to mean a very ordinary sort of strength and heartiness, compared with that of the divine archer. As to apologising for this final exaltation of our subject of the Monthly Nurse (which is a name that the 'sage and serious' Homer would not have scrupled to give to Diana herself, who was at once the *moon* and *midwife* of the ancient world), we shall no more think of doing it, than we should of blushing for the

45

very moonlight when it sheds its beams on the bed of some newly-blessed mother, and combines thoughts of angels with her cradle.

—— 'As the feet
Of the birth-speeding goddess touch'd the isle
The labour seiz'd Latona, and the hour
Was come. Around a palm-tree's stem she threw
Her linked arms, and press'd her bowed knees
On the soft meadow. Earth beneath her smiled,
And Phoebus leap'd to light. The goddesses
Scream'd in their joy. There, oh thou archer god!
Those goddesses imbathed thee in fair streams
With chaste and pure immersion; swathing thee
With new-wove mantle, white, of delicate folds,
Clasp'd with a golden belt. His mother's milk
Fed not Apollo of the golden sword;
But Themis with immortal hands infused
Nectar and bland ambrosia. Then rejoiced
Latona, that her boy had sprung to light
Valiant, and bearer of the bow; but when,
Oh Phoebus! thou hadst tasted with thy lips
Ambrosial food, the golden swathes no more
Withheld thee, panting; nor could bands restrain:
But every ligament was snapt in scorn.
Straight did Apollo stand in heaven, and face
Th' immortals. 'Give me,' cried the boy, 'a harp
And bending bow; and let me prophesy
To mortal man th' unerring will of Jove.'

Far-darting Phoebus of the flowing hair
Down from the broad-track'd mountain pass'd,and all
Those goddesses look'd on in ravish'd awe,
And all the Delian Isle was heap'd with gold,
So gladden'd by his presence the fair son
Of Jove and of Latona. For he chose
That island as his home o'er every isle
Or continent, and lov'd it as his soul.
It flourish'd like a mountain, when its top
Is hid with flowering blossoms of a wood.'

THE MONTHLY NURSE

What a mixture of force and beauty is in these pictures! How affecting is the graceful patience of the mother, and the gentle beauty of the landscape! And how noble, Apollo's suddenly 'standing in heaven;' and his descent down the mountain, striking the goddesses with awe, and showering golden light on the island, which from that day forth flourishes out of the sea, like his own luxuriant head of hair, or some woody *mountain-top in blossom!*

Yet the birth of the commonest human being is an event hardly less divine, if we think of all that he is destined to suffer and enjoy, and of his own immortal hopes. Here is a charming passage from Beaumont, which comes more home to us than these out-of-door maternities of the Pagan heaven, with all their beauty. A daughter is attended in child-birth by her mother, who has warranted a betrothment not yet sanctioned by the father: —

> *Violanta.* Mother, I'd not offend you: might not Gerrard
> Steal in, and see me in the evening ?
> *Angelina.*   Well,
> Bid him do so.
> *Viol.*   Heaven's blessing on your heart.
> Do you not call child-bearing *travel*, mother?
> *Angel.* Yes.
> *Viol.*   It may well be so. The bare-foot traveller
> That's born a prince, and walks his pilgrimage,
> Whose tender feet kiss the remorseless stones
> Only, ne'er felt a travel like to it.
> Alas, dear mother, you groan'd thus for me,
> And yet how disobedient have I been!
> *Angel.* Peace, Violanta: thou hast always been
> Gentle and good.
> *Viol.*   Gerrard is better, mother.
> * * * * * * * * I am now, methinks,
> Even in the laud of ease. I'll sleep.
> *Angel.* * * * * * * * * * * * * Silken rest
> Tie all thy cares up.

THE QUACK DOCTOR

What a pestilent knave is this same!
SHAKSPERE

THE QUACK DOCTOR

BY PAUL PRENDERGAST

The APOTHECARY having already appeared in this work, it may perhaps, be thought unnecessary to exhibit the Quack. We grant that these two artists have, in some respects, a strong mutual resemblance; yet, notwithstanding the opinion of several judicious persons, we cannot admit that they are as like one another as two peas. There may be that sort of likeness between them which there is between a bean and a pea — or, as it is called, a family one; but they also differ in many important particulars. They both pursue similar ends, real as well as apparent; for each, while he professes to cure diseases, is endeavouring to get money: but whereas the Quack is governed in his choice of means by downright knavery, the Apothecary is more than half influenced by the opposite cause of error. The one is no philosopher at all, and he partly believes in specifies; the other is a natural philosopher, and believes in nothing of the kind; but not being, in a practical sense at least, a moral one also, he does not hesitate to profess that he has discovered an universal medicine.

The Quack sometimes calls himself a medical dissenter; a term, the meaning of which is rendered somewhat ambiguous, by certain of his fraternity having of late thought proper to assume the title of Reverend. The word dissenter does not, however, necessarily imply that there is any peculiarity in his theological opinions, although that, and a pretence to excessive sanctity, will do little harm to one of his calling, either within or without the pale of the faculty. Medical dissent is to be understood to mean, a departure from the established faith as regards the art of healing; what that established faith is, and how much of truth there is in it to afford the champions of freedom of thought matter for denial, we need not stop to enquire. A belief prevails that there is something, at least, to dissent from; and the Quack, accordingly, obtains all due credit with a certain class for strength of mind, and honesty of intention — qualities from which contempt for authority is commonly supposed to proceed.

It is gratifying to reflect upon what is called the modem progress of mind — a topic which you will hardly find untouched even in a preface to a cookery book. Formerly, a fanatic preaching in a tub, could, by mere confidence and force of lungs, persuade the multitude to believe whatever he pleased, and a vagabond medicine-vender, haranguing the crowd from a stage, succeeded equally well, with similar resources. But now we have no leading by the nose, no wholesale cramming down the throat — nay, we have a praiseworthy disdain of relying on the good faith of our betters. Our intellect must be satisfied; we must be argued with; we must be convinced; — the Ranter must reason; the Quack must theorise. At present, we have nothing to say of the logic peculiar to the first of these professors; but it may be expected that we should give some notion of the philosophy usually propounded by the latter. The physiological and medical views of the Quack are sometimes set forth in a book, but more generally in an advertisement, and are then expressed much in the following manner: —

Principiis Obsta. — OVID

WHEN we consider the multifarious relations which the coexistent peculiarities incidental to the human frame and to the external world necessarily involve, we shall instantaneously perceive, that the physical mechanism of Man is liable to numerous diseases. It is unnecessary to expose, to an enlightened Public, the fallacies of a prejudiced faculty, in all their naked deformity; as the slightest reflection will immediately serve to exemplify their fatal results. There is but one medical theory on which the suffering valetudinarian, and reflective philanthropist, can repose with confidence and safety, and that one we shall (from benevolence rather than gain), endeavour to unfold. Universal correspondence to the characteristics of veracity is the only sure mark of truth; facts are stubborn things; and the never-failing success of the Universal Anticacoethic Pills stamps the unerring fiat of certitude on the unquestionable deductions of reason. Experiment and observation are strongly recommended

*by the illustrius Bacon; and, accordingly, a trial of the
Universal Anticacoethic Pills is earnestly solicited from
all those who are labouring under any of those diversified
ailments which obnubilate the chequered path of life.*

*Their composition is of the most innocuous description;
the deleterious qualities of the destructive mineral, and
the baneful essence of the poisonous herb, are alike
sedulously avoided; and the mild and genial operation of
the salutiferous vegetable, is the gentle but irresistible
power by which they eradicate disease from the ener-
vated system, restore the tone of the most dilapidated
stomach, and force conviction on the most sceptical mind.
According to the Anticacoethic theory, all diseases arise
from the Cacoethes (a term derived from the Greek, to
some of the philosophers of which country it is more than
probable that the secret was known), and until the Ca-
coethic virus is expelled the system, vain are the efforts of
the languishing sufferer to obtain a cure — an object
which the Universal Anticacoethic Pills alone are the
means calculated to effect. To prove the inviolable cor-
rectness of the Anticacoethic theory, it will be sufficient
to remark, that chylification is universally admitted to be
the* sine qua non *of the sanguiferos supply; and the
following letters from the late distinguished surgeon, Mr.
Abernethy, and his intimate friend, Dr. Baillie, preclude
comment, and necessitate assent.*

London, October 1, 1836.
*MY DEAR DICKSON, — I have tried your pills in a great
variety of cases, and am fully confident that they form an
admirable system for the cure of the majority of diseases.
I remain, &c., yours truly,*
To H U M Dickson, Esq. the Anticacoethist
JOHN ABERNETHY

London, July 4, 1820.
DEAR DICKSON, — Your pills are capital. They beat all others I ever tried; and I must beg you to send me another box, for I find them an invaluable treasure to my wife and family.

Believe, me, very sincerely yours,
To H U M Dickson Esq   MATTHEW BAILLIE, MD

The subjoined acknowledgment, which, while it demonstrates the superior efficacy of the Anticacoethic Pills, is highly gratifying to the feelings of Mr Dickson, was last week received by Mr D

Southampton, March 3, 1840.
HONOURED AND RESPECTED SIR, — How shall I find adequate words to address you? — my truest friend — my best benefactor — the preserver of my darling child! Yes, sir, thanks to your inestimable discovery, my little Neddy is at length restored to the almost blighted hopes of his anxious mother. But let me control my feelings, to detail, for the benefit of the incredulous, the astonishing effects of the Anticacoethic Pills. My little cherub, who is now in his sixth year, was attacked with a complaint in the inside, consisting of spasms, attended with the most heart-rending convulsions that can be possibly conceived. I took him to all the doctors I could think of, and had all sorts of things tried, but to no purpose; and, in the meantime, poor Edward became daily worse and worse, till at last he was so swelled, that he was nearly as broad as he was high, and his poor little eyes turned in towards the nose in such a degree, that I thought he would have been an object all his life; his mouth, too, became so dreadfuly widened and distorted, that I have cried for hours at the thought of it. The doctors now gave him over, and declared nothing could save him, when, as a last resource, I determined to try the Anticacoethic Pills. Finding that their immediate effect was a decrease in the

symptoms, I persevered in their use, and, at the end of a fortnight, my little prattler had perfectly recovered. Oh! Mr D, pardon a mother's fondness; but had you — could you have — witnessed the happy restoration of my beloved child, what heartfelt satisfaction would have beamed in your features, at a sight of so affecting a nature, and also at the splendid triumph of the Universal Anticacoethic Pills, so unequivocally exemplified in the foregoing instance! You are at liberty to make whatever use you like of this communication; and oh! Mr. Dickson, believe me to remain, with feelings of the liveliest gratitude.

Ever sincerely yours,
MARTHA STACEY.

To H U M Dickson, Esq, inventor of the Anticacoethic Pills

Sold by H. U. M. Dickson, at the New Anticacoethic Institution, Bridge-street, Blackfriars, where also may be had the following works — Doctorial Dulness, or a Fig for the Faculty; The Life Preserver; The Rational Physician; The Triumph of Truth; and various other productions by the same author.

Sold also at the Branch Institution, Red Lion Square, Holborn; and by all respectable Medicine Venders in town and country. Be particular in asking for Dickson's Universal Anticacoethic Pills; none others are genuine; and likewise in observing the government stamp upon the box, to counterfeit which is felony.

Mr. Dickson attends daily at the Anticacoethic Institution, from 10 to 4, to give gratuitous advice to the afflicted. All letters from the country, minutely describing the case, and containing a remittance, punctually attended to. Medicines forwarded to all parts of the world, and carefully packed and sealed, to prevent observation.

Swift, in describing the conversion of Mr. Edmand Curll to Judaism, says, 'They then spoke to him in the Hebrew tongue, which he not understanding, it was observed, had great weight with him.' There is, even now, a sufficient number of such people as Mr Curll in the world, to make talking Hebrew to them, or what, in effect, is much the same, abundantly worth the while of an impostor. The reasoning, too, which is least intelligible, is, of necessity, the most unanswerable. Not that the Quack addresses, or would be wise in addressing, utter and unmixed nonsense to his dupes. Advertiser, writer, lecturer, or whatever he may be, he puts forward, every here and there, some common-place truism, in such a form of words that his meaning may just be guessed at, by which artifice he gets credit for profundity with the vulgar, and, at the same time, causes a great deal to be taken on trust which is either entirely false and absurd, or else, which is more frequently the case, has no signification whatever. Nor is the Quack altogether a systematic coiner of fine words. They seem natural to him, as, indeed, they do to all his kindred, amongst whom advertising tailors and drapers may with great propriety be reckoned. These glib and oily words — these 'genteel expressions' — in which we are sure that the swindler even *thinks*, serve as effectually to conceal his knavery, as his 'fashionable exterior' does to disguise his person. Wherever we meet with them, we suspect humbug, either wilful or involuntary. An advertisement (now before us) about a cosmetic, describes it as 'a mild and innocent preparation, from beautiful exotics. It effectually eradicates eruptions, tan, pimples, freckles, redness, spots, and all cutaneous imperfections; renders the most sallow complexion delicately fair, clear, and delightfully soft — imparting a healthy juvenile bloom, as well as *realising* a delicate white neck, hand, and arm.' Faugh! Another nasty puff, of the same kind, speaks of the nipping easterly winds as being 'so prejudicial to the hands of the *superior classes*.' The man must have licked the blarney stone to some purpose, to write in this way.

The modern Quack is a great cultivator of manners and appearance. Formerly, it was the custom of these gentry to dress like scarecrows, in order that they might he taken for men of learning; but now their apparel, with the exception of some slight touch of eccentricity — such, for instance, as a fur collar, which gives them what some folks are pleased to call a *distingué* appearance — only differs from that of the rest of the world in being rather more fine. This is more especially the case with those who belong, as not a few of them do, to the Israelitish persuasion, such Quacks being remarkable, generally, at least, for large shirt pins, conspicuous watchguards, numerous finger rings, and polished boots. To this class divers of the advertising 'surgeon dentists' belong.

The Quack — we are still speaking of the Medical Quack — is not always an inventor, compounder, or retailer of patent medicines. He is sometimes a Homoeopathist; or a pretender to cure diseases by Animal Magnetism; or an itinerant lecturer on Phrenology; or, it may be, all three together, and, under the rose, an Astrologer into the bargain, who describes characters and tells fortunes at so much per booby, to the no small annoyance of all those who, with many reasonable men, consider that the brain is something more than mere stuffing, and would have no means neglected of discovering its use. He is also pretty sure to entertain new views in morals, whereof community of property (which would be a very convenient arrangement personally to himself) is always one of the chief. Moreover, he is an universal philanthropist, bitterly inveighing against the oppression practised by those in power, and the ignorance and superstition of the clergy. When he has been shewn up in a paper or a review, he takes great care to compare his own case to that of various philosophers who have suffered for their opinions, never failing to descant particularly on Galileo and the Inquisition. This fellow is a genius — a sort of Crichton in his way — and is often clever enough to pass himself off for a foreign count, rivalled though he may be, in his respectable vocation, by some who have a real claim to that dignity.

There is a certain saying about persons who deceive the public, so old that we need only hint at it. We do not, however, imagine that the Quack is, in any measure, the dupe of his own imposture, unless when he arrives at extreme old age, a time when those who have told lies all their lives, sometimes end by believing them. 'If,' said a very celebrated one, and a foreigner to boot, 'you wish to succeed wid de English beeble, you must dell dem someding dat common sense shew to be imborsible.' In our opinion, the rogue concocts advertisements, forges commendatory letters, and fabricates cases, on principles, and with feelings, precisely similar to those with which an angler makes an artificial fly, or a schoolboy sets a springe. The patients, of course, are the trout and woodcocks — were it sportsman-like to say so, we would rather call them gulls and gudgeons: — and be it observed, that a bread pill, in a literal sense, is no bad bait for the latter.

We much regret that we are obliged to condense into so short a space the interesting life and adventures of Mr. Jacob Diddams, and to confine ourselves to a brief notice of their leading points. Diddams was born in London, though in what alley we cannot take upon ourselves precisely to say. It is certain, however, that his father was a barber; and that his mother, a Miss Jacob, was connected with a very numerous, and somewhat ancient, family of that name, many of the members of which had resided for some time in the neighbourhood of the Commercial Road. It appears, also, that soon after the birth of young Jacob, his parents became suddenly possessed of some property, in consequence of the death of a relation on his mother's side. He was sent, at the usual age, to school, where, it is related of him, that he had a remarkable power of persuading his playmates of the truth of the most evident falsehoods. Amongst other things, he managed to make a thick-headed farmer's son believe that he had a pop-gun that would carry a mile, and further, to induce the lout to purchase the toy of him, at the moderate price of five shillings. The circumstance which, there is every reason to suppose, determined the bent of his genius, and which took place before he had completed his twelfth year, deserves to be recorded. He one day observed his father suffering severely from an attack of the gout, and on enquiring why he did not take some drops then in much repute for the cure of that distemper, had the nature of a quack medicine explained to him. 'So, then,' said Jacob, 'if I were to roll up so many bits of putty, and spend enough money in advertising them, I should make my fortune.' His future course of life was settled on that day.

At the death of his father, which put him in possession of a tolerable sum, Jacob Diddams had arrived at years which, were honesty really the best policy, might have been called years of discretion. He was now enabled to carry his long-cherished scheme into execution; he did so; he was successful; and the elixir which bore his name, or rather his assumed one, was held for a long time in such estimation, as has not been since exceeded by any similar compound.

The pleasure derived from the practice of Quackery is not owing merely to the emolument which it produces: the genuine Quack delights also in his occupation for its own sake. Mr Jacob Diddams devoted those hours of leisure which were permitted to him by his professional pursuits to the amusement of field-preaching — an exercise in which he soon obtained great proficiency. For many years he was well known (as a divine, not as a physician) on Kennington Common. He is likewise said to have made considerable progress in the unknown tongues, but to have desisted from the further cultivation of them, in consequence of their pretensions being exploded.

Mr Diddams never had much more faith in Methodism than he had in medicine, and he has lately not only renounced his former creed, but also every other. He is now a lecturer at a Social Institution; and, as he is somewhat advancing in years, it is probable that he believes to a certain extent in the principles which he expounds. He has not yet been called upon to contribute his possessions to the common stock, nobody having any suspicion of his enormous wealth, which he is at much pains to conceal, never venturing among his new disciples with anything on his back worth stealing, or with more money in his pocket than the change for a sixpence.

There is a question, often suggested by the advertisement sheet of a newspaper to ourselves, which we would fain submit to the reader. The government derives an immense revenue from the sale of patent medicines: — How many simpletons are there in the United Kingdom? But, we are now touching on a matter about which a jest is out of place. Do we not continually meet, in the public prints, with cases in which people are *poisoned by* the administration of some pernicious nostrum, and that not at once, as in common murders, but by slow, tedious, and painful degrees? In what position, then, do our legislators place themselves by the encouragement which, in licensing cart loads of deadly rubbish, they persist in giving to a set of wholesale corrupters of the public health — nay, of deliberate and sordid assassins

— for such are those, who, with their eyes open to the consequences, scatter poison abroad for the sake of gain? Let us not be told that these compounds are ascertained to be harmless before a sanction is given to their sale. No remedy whatever is so, if injudiciously taken. Nothing but extreme and deplorable ignorance can exonerate the patrons of quackery from the guilt of participating in murder. Politics are, of course, excluded from these pages, as they are from general society; but, wherever we may be, we have a right to complain of a public nuisance. The most extreme Tory, and the most violent Radical, agree in a regard for life and health. No honest man will dispute the assertion, that the system of granting patents to the manufacturers of a parcel of villanous trash, ought to be at once and totally abolished. The protection afforded to these scoundrels, is injustice to the medical profession — injustice, which is only equalled by the imbecility of extending it. What can possibly be the use of preserving the public from the incompetent Physician, and of abandoning it, at the same time, to the unprincipled nostrum vendor: of defending it from the fool, and betraying it to the knave? A man would do a wise thing, indeed, in barring his windows against thieves, and leaving his doors wide open. It is idle to plead the imperfect state of medicine, as an excuse for the abominable indifference, on the part of the legislature, to the rights of its practitioners. That science is imperfect, because its pursuit is discouraged. One thing, however, is certain; namely, that those whose calling it is should strenuously exert themselves to disprove the imputation on their skill, to which the patronage of empiricism by the state is equivalent. Another thing is equally certain; that there are quacks in the art of government, as well as in other matters, and that the constitution of individuals is not the only one which is tampered with. We hear much of remodelling institutions, reforming abuses, converting mechanics into moral philosophers, charity-school boys into theologians, and blackamoors into prodigies of piety; and, in the meantime, here is a crying and a flagrant nuisance unattended to, and almost unthought of. The imaginations of our rulers are running riot amid the perfumed groves of Utopia, and there is a pig-sty under their noses. — Away with it! It is now high time that law-makers should work, instead of talking — unless they are content to leave their craft still open to the reproach cast upon it by Johnson, who said that politics were now merely the means of rising in the world. Let them begin with the reformation of their own fraternity; let them get rid of quack politicians, and we shall not much longer be troubled with the QUACK DOCTOR.

AUTHORS AND ARTISTS

'**Paul Prendergast**'was the pseudonym used by **Percival Leigh 1813-1889** He qualified as a doctor, but soon abandoned medicine for a literary career. Like several others involved with 'Heads of the People', he wrote for 'Punch', and as an amateur actor he performed with Jerrold, Dickens and others. One of his works was 'Paul Prendergast, or the Comic Schoolmaster' 1859.

(**James Henry**) **Leigh Hunt 1784-1859**, writer and editor, wrote his first poems while a scholar at Christ's Hospital. He and his brother, John, collaborated on ventures including 'The Examiner', a political weekly. At one point they edited this from prison, having been prosecuted for an attack on the Prince Regent in its pages. His son, Thornton Leigh Hunt, also contributed to 'Heads of the People'

Richard Henry (or Hengist) Horne 1803-1884 was educated at Sandhurst, but instead of pursuing a military career, enlisted as a midshipman in the Mexican navy. In his long career as a writer, he contributed to numerous periodicals, and wrote several books and plays, including a life of Napoleon. In the 1850's he travelled to Australia, where he had little success in the goldfields, but subsequently became, among other things, a Chief of Mounted Police, and a champion swimmer.

(**Joseph**) **Kenny Meadows 1790-1874** The illustrations for 'Heads of the People' established Kenny Meadows' popularity as an artist. He produced illustrations for Punch, the Illustrated London News and a number of books. Many of these were in conjunction with Douglas Jerrold and other contributors to 'Heads of the People'.

Orrin Smith 1799-1842 Originally trained as an architect, Orrin Smith turned to wood engraving, and worked with Kenny Meadows and other artists. One of his last projects was Meadows' illustrated edition of Shakespeare, which he worked on until a few months before his death.

www.ingramcontent.com/pod-product-compliance
Lightning Source LLC
Chambersburg PA
CBHW060641280326
41933CB00012B/2101